# COLUMBUS

—Other titles in the Great Explorers of the World series—

# HENRY HUDSON
## Discoverer of the Hudson River
ISBN-13: 978-1-59845-123-8
ISBN-10:    1-59845-123-5

# MAGELLAN
## First to Circle the Globe
ISBN-13: 978-1-59845-097-2
ISBN-10:    1-59845-097-2

# HERNANDO DE SOTO
## Spanish Conquistador
## in the Americas
ISBN-13: 978-1-59845-104-7
ISBN-10:    1-59845-104-9

# MARCO POLO
## Amazing Adventures
## in China
ISBN-13: 978-1-59845-103-0
ISBN-10:    1-59845-103-0

# LA SALLE
## French Explorer
## of the Mississippi
ISBN-13: 978-1-59845-098-9
ISBN-10:    1-59845-098-0

# VASCO DA GAMA
## Discovering the
## Sea Route to India
ISBN-13: 978-1-59845-127-6
ISBN-10:    1-59845-127-8

# COLUMBUS

## Great Explorers of the World

# Opening Up the New World

**Stephen Feinstein**

**Enslow Publishers, Inc.**
40 Industrial Road
Box 398
Berkeley Heights, NJ 07922
USA

http://www.enslow.com

**Library of Congress Cataloging-in-Publication Data**

Feinstein, Stephen.
  Columbus : opening up the new world / Stephen Feinstein.
    p. cm. — (Great explorers of the world)
  Includes bibliographical references and index.
  Summary: "Examines the life of Italian explorer Christopher Columbus, including his
birth and early sea voyages, his famed discovery of the New World, and his legacy in
American history"—Provided by publisher.
  ISBN-13: 978-1-59845-101-6
  ISBN-10: 1-59845-101-4
  1.  Columbus, Christopher—Juvenile literature. 2.  Explorers—America—Biography—
Juvenile literature. 3.  Explorers—Spain—Biography—Juvenile literature. 4.  Explorers—
Italy—Biography—Juvenile literature. 5.  America—Discovery and exploration—Spanish—
Juvenile literature. 6.  America—Discovery and exploration—Italian—Juvenile literature.
I. Title.
  E111.F28 2009
  970.01'5092—dc22
  [B]

                              2008038633


Printed in the United States of America

10 9 8 7 6 5 4 3 2 1

**To Our Readers:** We have done our best to make sure all Internet Addresses in this book were
active and appropriate when we went to press. However, the author and the publisher have no
control over and assume no liability for the material available on those Internet sites or on other
Web sites they may link to. Any comments or suggestions can be sent by e-mail to
comments@enslow.com or to the address on the back cover.

♻ Enslow Publishers, Inc., is committed to printing our books on recycled paper. The paper in
every book contains 10% to 30% post-consumer waste (PCW). The cover board on the outside
of each book contains 100% PCW. Our goal is to do our part to help young people and the
environment too!

**Illustration Credits:** Associated Press, p. 102; Bridgeman-Giraudon / Art Resource, NY,
p. 33; Enslow Publishers, Inc., p. 58; Everett Collection, p. 43; The Granger Collection, New
York, pp. 3, 10, 18–19, 66–67, 72–73, 76, 98–99; © Jupiterimages Corporation, pp. 17, 64;
Keystone / Eyedea / Everett Collection, p. 59; Library of Congress, pp. 46–47, 57, 68, 69,
82–83, 101; Scala / Art Resource, NY, pp. 24–25, 78; © Shutterstock®, pp. 13, 28–29, 104.

**Ship Illustration Used in Chapter Openers:** © Jupiterimages Corporation.

**Cover Illustration:** The Granger Collection, New York (Portrait of Christopher Columbus).

# Contents

# EXPLORER TIMELINE

**1451**—Christopher Columbus is born sometime between August 25 and October 31 in Genoa, Italy.

**1461**—Columbus's first experiences at sea.
**–1469**

**1474**—Makes his first long sea journey to the Greek island of Chios.

**1476**—Columbus sails aboard *Bechalla* in commercial fleet bound for England; *Bechalla* burns and sinks during attack; Columbus makes it to shore at the Portuguese village of Lagos.

**1477**—Columbus sails to England, Ireland, and Iceland; settles in Lisbon.

**1479**—Marries Felipa Moniz Perestrello.

**1480**—Columbus and Felipa move to the island of Porto
**or 1481**  Santo.

**1482**—Columbus sails to Ghana and Guinea on the west-
**–1484**  ern coast of Africa.

**1484**—Presents his Enterprise of the Indies proposal to Portugal's King John II, who rejects it.

**1485**—Columbus and his son, Diego, move to Spain.

**1486**—Presents his proposal to King Ferdinand and Queen Isabella; the Spanish monarchs show some interest but make no commitment.

**1487**—Ferdinand and Isabella reject Columbus's proposal.

**1488**—Columbus presents proposal again to King John II of Portugal, who once more rejects the plan; Beatriz de Arana gives birth to Columbus's second son, Ferdinand, in August.

**1492**—*January 2:* Ferdinand and Isabella's Christian army finally defeats the caliphate of Granada, the last Muslim stronghold in Spain.

—*April 17:* Columbus signs a contract with Ferdinand and Isabella for his first voyage.

—*August 3:* Sets sail from Palos, Spain. His fleet consists of the *Niña*, the *Pinta*, and the *Santa Maria*.

—*September 6:* Columbus's fleet departs the Canary Islands.

—*October 12:* Lands on an island in the present-day Bahamas, his first stop in what will become known as "the New World"; names the island San Salvador; encounters the Arawak Indians, who call their island Guanahaní.

1493—*March 15:* Columbus returns to Palos, Spain; Ferdinand and Isabella name Columbus "Admiral of the Ocean Sea" and make him governor of all islands in the Caribbean.

—*September 25:* Sets sail on second voyage from Cadiz, Spain.

1496—Columbus returns to Spain.

1498—*May 30:* Sets sail on his third voyage from Seville, Spain.

*August 5:* Columbus or some of his men set foot on coast of Venezuela.

1500—Columbus returns to Spain in chains; Ferdinand and Isabella free him but do not restore his titles.

1502—*May 9:* Sets sail on his fourth voyage from Cadiz, Spain. Columbus and his crew are shipwrecked near Jamaica in December.

1504—*August 13:* Columbus and crew are rescued and arrive in Santo Domingo, Hispaniola.

—*September 12:* Columbus arrives back in Spain.

—*November 16:* Queen Isabella dies.

1506—*May 20:* Columbus dies in Valladolid, Spain.

# Chapter 1

# The First Sight of Land

In August 1492, a little fleet sailed westward across the uncharted waters of the Ocean Sea (today known as the Atlantic Ocean). Christopher Columbus, a bold Italian navigator, commanded the fleet, which consisted of the *Niña*, the *Pinta*, and the *Santa Maria*. Columbus sailed aboard the flagship, the *Santa Maria*. Captain Vincente Yáñez Pinzón commanded the *Niña*, while his brother Martín Alonso Pinzón captained the *Pinta*.

Columbus had convinced Spain's King Ferdinand and Queen Isabella to finance the voyage. He had promised to bring them a huge treasure of gold and spices. What would turn out to be the most momentous voyage of discovery in world history had begun on August 3, 1492. That day, Columbus's fleet set sail from Palos, Spain. Columbus hoped to reach the Indies.

He had read descriptions of these fabled eastern lands in the reports of Marco Polo, the Venetian trader. Polo had made the overland journey from Europe to China at the end of the thirteenth century. He had explored many different regions of Asia. Columbus was so

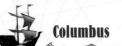 

Christopher Columbus's fleet was composed of the *Niña*, *Pinta*, and *Santa María*.

impressed by Polo's exploits that he carried the Venetian's book with him aboard the *Santa Maria*. Columbus believed that sailing west would prove to be the shortest route to the Indies. If he were successful, fame and fortune would follow.

In his journal entry of August 3, 1492, Columbus wrote: "We set sail on this third day of August, 1492, at 8 o'clock in the morning, from the bar of Saltes. The wind is strong and variable, and we had gone 45 miles to the south by sunset. After dark I altered course for the Canary Islands, to the SW and south be west."[1]

## SIGNS OF LAND?

At the Canary Islands—off the west coast of Africa—Columbus had a new rudder built for the *Pinta*. He also had the *Niña*'s triangular sails replaced by square-rigged sails, like those on the other two ships. Caravels, small sailing ships, such as the *Pinta* and the *Niña*, were usually rigged with triangular sails. But Columbus felt that square-rigged sails could better withstand the strong winds he expected to encounter.

On September 6, 1492, Columbus's fleet departed from Gomera on the Canary Islands. Three days later, the fleet had left all sight of land behind. In his journal entry of September 9, 1492, Columbus wrote: "This day we completely lost sight of land, and many men sighed and wept for fear they would not see it again for a long time. I comforted them with great promises of lands and riches."[2] Columbus decided that from then on, he would not tell the crew the true distance they had come each day. He would keep accurate records for himself. But he kept a separate record for the crew, reporting shorter distances so as to lessen their anxiety. For example, in his journal entry of September 10, Columbus wrote: "Today I made 180 miles at a speed of 7 1/2 knots.

I recorded only 144 miles in order not to alarm the sailors if the voyage is lengthy."[3]

By September 17, the fleet entered an area of the Atlantic Ocean filled with floating weeds, known as the Sargasso Sea. Columbus took the weeds as evidence that land was nearby. In his journal for that date, Columbus wrote:

> . . . I saw a great deal of weed today—weed from rocks that lie to the west. I take this to mean that we are near land. The weed resembles stargrass, except that it has long stalks and shoots and is loaded with fruit like the mastic tree. Some of this weed looks like river grass, and the crew found a live crab in a patch of it. This is a sure sign of land, for crabs are not found even 240 miles from shore. . . . Everyone is cheerful, and the *Pinta*, the fastest sailing vessel, went ahead as fast as it could in order to sight land. . . . This morning I also saw another ringtail—a white bird with a long plumed tail—a bird that is not accustomed to sleeping on the sea.[4]

For the next several days, as the fleet sailed through patches of weeds, Columbus noticed several other things that he believed were surely signs of land. These included a particular cloud bank on September 18, and a windless drizzle on September 19. On September 21, Columbus wrote that they had encountered a whale, "which is another sign of land, for whales always stay near the coast."[5]

This is a replica of the *Santa María*, one of Columbus's ships.

## MUTINY IN THE AIR

During the next few days, Columbus began to worry that he might have problems with his crew. Tensions were rising on all three ships. They had already come a very long way from Spain. They were at least 1,800 miles out into a great ocean that seemed to have no end. Despite all of the apparent signs of land, so far they had not found any. And there were no guarantees that they would ever be able to reach home again.

On September 22, the winds blowing from the west pleased Columbus. He wrote that ". . . these contrary winds are very helpful because the crew is agitated, thinking that no winds blow in these parts that will return them to Spain."[6]

On September 24, Columbus wrote in his journal:

> I am having serious trouble with the crew, despite the signs of land that we have and those given to us by Almighty God. In fact, the more God shows the men manifest signs that we are near land, the more their impatience and inconstancy increases. . . . All day long and all night long those who are awake and able to get together never cease to talk to each other in circles, complaining that they will never be able to return home. They have said that it is insanity and suicidal on their part to risk their lives following the madness of a foreigner. They have said that not only am I willing to risk my life just to become a great Lord, but that I have

deceived them to further my ambition. . . . Some feel that they have already arrived where men have never dared to sail and that they are not obliged to go to the end of the world, especially if they are delayed anymore and will not have sufficient provisions to return. I am told by a few trusted men (and these are few in number!) that if I persist in going onward, the best course of action will be to throw me into the sea some night.[7]

Columbus was afraid that his crew might very well decide to stage a mutiny. After all, they were all Spaniards. They might believe that because Columbus was a foreigner, an Italian, they could get away with it.

In the same journal entry, Columbus wrote that he did not trust the Pinzón brothers. He believed the crewmen were taking their complaints to the Pinzóns and that the two captains sided with the sailors. Also, Martín Alonso Pinzón, the captain of the *Pinta*, had been racing far ahead of the other two ships. Columbus assumed that Martín Alonso Pinzón wanted to be the first to sight land, thus stealing that honor from Columbus. And then if Columbus just happened to disappear beneath the water, the riches and glory from any discoveries would belong to Pinzón. Despite his lingering distrust, Columbus knew that his life, and the success of the voyage depended on the continued loyalty of the Pinzón brothers. So Columbus did what he could to convince them that their best chance for a successful outcome of the voyage was to follow his command.

At sunset the very next day, Martín Alonso Pinzón called out from the *Pinta* that he saw land. He claimed the reward Columbus had promised to the first man to sight land. In his journal entry of September 25, Columbus wrote: "The crew of the *Niña* all climbed the mast and rigging, and all claimed that it was land. At the moment I myself was sure that it was land and reckoned that it was about 75 miles to the SW."[8] But the next morning, Columbus wrote: "After sunrise I realized that what we all thought was land last evening was nothing more than squall clouds, which often resemble land."[9] Columbus and his crew still had many more miles to sail.

On October 7, there was another false sighting of land. In his journal for that date, Columbus wrote: ". . . the *Niña*, which is a better sailer, ran ahead and fired a cannon and ran up a flag on her mast to indicate that land had been sighted. Joy turned to dismay as the day progressed, for by evening we had found no land and had to face the reality that it was only an illusion."[10]

Three days later, Columbus again detected a feeling of mutiny in the air. In his journal entry for October 10, Columbus described the growing impatience of his crewmen and how he dealt with it. Columbus wrote in his journal:

They grumbled and complained of the long voyage, and I reproached them for their lack of spirit, telling them that, for better or worse, they had to complete the enterprise. . . . I cheered them on as best as I could, telling them of all the honors and rewards they were about to receive. I also told the men that it was useless to complain, for I had started out to find the Indies and would continue until I had accomplished that mission, with the help of Our Lord.[11]

To avoid a mutiny, Columbus asked his crew to wait three more days to see if they would sight land.

This painting by William J. Aylward shows the landing of Columbus in the New World in 1492.

But according to the testimony years later by various members of the crew, Columbus may have told the men something else. Apparently he believed that they were indeed very close to land. He asked that the crew allow him three more days to find land. If by that time they still had not sighted land, Columbus promised he would turn back. Other accounts give yet another version of events. Columbus himself wanted to turn back, but he was encouraged not to give up by the Pinzón brothers. Historians do not know which story holds the most truth.

If there is any truth to the three-day deadline version, then the timing of the first sighting of land is indeed amazing. In any event, no matter which story is true, on the night of October 11, Columbus thought he saw a strange light in the distance. In his journal for that date, he wrote:

About 10 o'clock at night, while standing on the sterncastle, I thought I saw a light to the west. It looked like a little wax candle bobbing up and down. It had the same appearance as a light or torch belonging to fishermen or travelers who alternately raised and lowered it, or perhaps were going from house to house. I am the first to admit that I was so eager to find land that I did not trust my own senses. . . . Then, at two hours after midnight, the *Pinta* fired a cannon, my prearranged signal for the sighting of land.[12]

## "LAND! LAND!"

According to Columbus, Rodrigo de Triana, also called Juan Rodríguez Bermejo, a lookout on the *Pinta*, was the first to sight land. At 2:00 A.M. on October 12, 1492, Bermejo saw a line of low white cliffs shimmering in the distance in the moonlight. He cried out "*Tierra*! *Tierra*!," which in Spanish means "Land! Land!"

Columbus was eager to go ashore. After five weeks at sea, he and all the men of the three ships were thrilled at finally making landfall. They had arrived at an island in the Bahamas. As they stepped ashore, Columbus carried the royal banner, while the Pinzón brothers carried banners decorated with green crosses and letters representing Ferdinand and Isabella. After a prayer of thanksgiving, Columbus took possession of the island for the king and queen of Spain. He named the island San Salvador ("Holy Savior").

# Chapter 2

# Early Years at Sea

**Many** historians refer to Columbus by different names. Christopher Columbus is the English translation of his Italian birth name, Cristoforo Colombo. Some historians use the name Cristóbal Colón, the name Columbus used when he lived in Spain. And when he lived in Portugal, Columbus used the name Christovão Colom.

Christopher Columbus was born in Genoa, Italy, most likely between August 25 and October 31, 1451. Like much of Columbus's early life, there is very little documentation to verify places and dates. This is not unusual when researching a person who lived so long ago. In those days, unless and until the person became famous, written records were often sporadic or even nonexistent. As a result, some historians believe Columbus may have come not from Genoa but from Corsica. Others have traced his origin to Greece. Yet others claim he was either Spanish, Portuguese, French, or Polish, and possibly half-Jewish. However, most historians accept Genoa as Columbus's place of birth. In a 1498 will, Columbus

wrote, "I being born in Genoa" and "Genoa . . . in it I was born."[1]

## FIRST GLIMPSES OF THE SEA

Christopher Columbus was the eldest son of Domenico Columbus and Susanna Fontanarossa. He had three younger brothers, Bartholomew, Giovanni Pellegrino, and Giacomo, and one sister, Bianchinetta. Domenico Columbus was a weaver

This view of the Italian port city Genoa was painted by an anonymous artist in the fifteenth century.

of wool, a craftsman, and merchant. His wool shop was on the ground floor of the Columbus family home in Genoa.

Young Christopher was educated in the primary school of the Wool Merchants Guild. There he studied religion, arithmetic, geography, and some navigation. Because Genoa was a major Mediterranean seaport and center of trade, the boys needed to learn navigation. Genoa was on a

narrow strip of land along the coast below a range of mountains. There was not much land available for farming, so the open sea offered the most promising future for Genoese youth.

When Christopher was old enough, he worked in his father's wool shop. But he was not interested enough in wool processing and selling to plan a future in the family business. Even as a young child, Christopher must have seen the sea. And he must have smelled the salt air. Perhaps he wandered along the docks. Or he may have walked on the beach.

The harbor at Genoa was constantly filled with the comings and goings of ships from all over the Mediterranean and beyond. Sailors on the docks spoke the languages of many different countries. These were the sights and sounds that worked their way into the imagination of young Christopher. The sea beckoned as the gateway to adventure.

According to Columbus scholar Samuel Eliot Morison, "Genoa was certainly a place to give any active lad a hankering for sea adventure."[2] English sailor Ernle Bradford added, "It was in fact more than natural that one of the world's greatest sailors should come from Genoa."[3]

## YOUTHFUL ADVENTURES AT SEA

Christopher Columbus first went to sea at a very early age. Many men of seafaring communities, such as Genoa, fished for a living. Even those who worked on shore would go fishing in their spare time. Each family either owned or had access to a small sailboat. Domenico Columbus probably took young Christopher fishing. When Christopher had learned to sail, his father probably sent him along the coast to buy wool, wine, and cheeses, and to sell cloth.

According to Columbus's conflicting statements later in life, his first experience aboard a sailing ship occurred either in 1461, when he was ten, or in 1469, when he was eighteen. In a letter to the king and queen of Spain in 1501, Columbus wrote: "At a very tender age I entered upon the sea sailing, and so have I continued to this day. That art [of navigation] inclines him who follows it to want to know the secrets of this world. Already 40 years have passed that I have been in this employment."[4] But in an entry in his journal dated December 21, 1492, Columbus wrote: "I have followed the sea for 23 years without leaving it for any time worth reckoning."[5] Yet another date comes from Columbus's son Ferdinand, who reported that Christopher Columbus began his seagoing career at the age of fourteen.

At first, Christopher worked on various ships as a common sailor and a messenger. He learned the essential skills of a seaman, including even more about navigation. In 1470, Domenico relocated

The port of Genoa, Italy
as it appears today.

his family and business to Savona, a seaport several miles from Genoa. There he set up a new wool shop. In the following years, whenever Christopher was not working on a ship, he would help out in his father's shop.

In 1474, Christopher Columbus made his first long voyage at sea to the Greek island of Chios in the Aegean Sea. The ship was owned by Genoese merchants who had a monopoly of trade with that Greek island. Chios was a bustling center of trade. In the island's busy bazaars and shops, merchants from eastern Asia, or "the East," exchanged their goods with those from Europe, or "the West." Influenced by the displays of silks, pearls, precious stones, and intoxicating spices, Columbus fell under the spell of the East. He realized that a great fortune could be made in trade with merchants in the East.

In the summer of 1476, when Columbus was twenty-five, he set sail as a seaman aboard a Flemish vessel called *Bechalla*. The ship was part of an armed commercial expedition organized in Genoa. *Bechalla* was one of five ships in the small fleet bound for England. This voyage was to become the adventure that would change the course of Christopher Columbus's life. For the first time in his life, Columbus sailed through the Strait of Gibraltar and out into the open Atlantic, then known as the Ocean Sea. On August 13, 1476, the fleet was sailing between Cape Santa Maria and Cape St. Vincent near the southern tip of Portugal. Suddenly, a fleet of at least thirteen French pirate ships attacked the Genoese fleet. In the ensuing battle, Columbus was wounded and ended up floating in the ocean. Three ships in the Genoese fleet, including *Bechalla*, were burned and sunk. Four large pirate ships were also sunk.

Columbus paddled toward shore, six miles away, while clinging to a piece of wreckage. Finally, he and some of the other men were rescued by fishermen from the Portuguese village of Lagos. Just by chance, Columbus had arrived in the backyard of Dom Henrique, also known as Henry the Navigator. Henry the Navigator's headquarters had been at nearby Sagres. Columbus may not have previously known about the great navigator and his accomplishments. But he would certainly have heard the myths, tales, and legends about Henry from the local fishermen of Lagos.

Henry the Navigator had participated in the conquest of Ceuta, the North African Muslim city at the Strait of Gibraltar, in 1415. The spices, jewels, and gold he saw there filled him with dreams of overseas exploration. In 1419, with support from King John I of Portugal, Henry founded a navigation school specializing in mapmaking, instrument making, and shipbuilding. Soon Portuguese sea captains, financed by Henry, began

sailing down the coast of West Africa. In 1434, they reached the northern edge of an African desert called the Sahara. By 1444, they sailed as far south as Cape Verde. They had discovered and colonized the seven islands of the Azores, the Madeira group of islands, and the Cape Verde Islands.

The Portuguese learned new techniques for covering greater distances at sea. Borrowing ideas about hull and sail designs from the Arabs, they developed a new type of ship called a caravel. Using the small, light, nimble caravels, the Portuguese learned how to sail hundreds of miles west of the African coast before catching the trade winds that carried them back in a wide loop. These tactics would enable the Portuguese to sail as far south as the Congo by 1480.

By the time of Henry's death in 1460, the Portuguese had established a series of trading posts along the coast of West Africa. They traded for ivory, gold, and slaves. The Portuguese used African slaves to work on sugar plantations in the Cape Verde Islands, off the coast of West Africa. The Portuguese traders established successful trading relations with various West African kingdoms. They had learned that a peaceful approach worked better for building wealth than attempting violent conquests.

Henry the Navigator financed many Portuguese expeditions to the West African Coast in the fifteenth century.

The tales of Henry the Navigator and other Portuguese voyages of exploration must have made a lasting impression on Christopher Columbus. The young Genoese seaman intended to learn as much as he could about the Portuguese and their many discoveries. Although weak from his wounds, Columbus traveled from Lagos to Lisbon. There, a kind member of the local Genoese community of merchants and shipbuilders offered him hospitality.

By February 1477, Columbus had regained his strength, and his wounds had healed. His thirst for adventure was stronger than ever. So he sailed on a commercial vessel from Lisbon to London. From there, he went to Bristol. He next sailed from Bristol to Galway, on the west coast of Ireland. From Galway, Columbus sailed in a fleet bound for Iceland. In Iceland, Columbus most likely heard about Greenland and the Vikings from Icelandic sailors. But it was not a place that interested him. The last ship to go from Iceland to the Norse settlements in Greenland did so in 1408. After several unusually mild centuries, the climate of Greenland had once again become too cold for settlement.

Regarding his travels in 1477, Columbus wrote:

> I sailed in the year 1477, in the month of February,
> a hundred leagues beyond the island of *Tile* [Thule

or Ultima Thule, which meant Iceland], . . . And to this island, which is as big as England, come English with their merchandise, especially they of Bristol. And at the season when I was there the sea was not frozen, but the tides were so great that in some places they rose 26 *braccia* [a Genoese *braccio* was equivalent to 22.9 inches], and fell as much in depth.[6]

## COLUMBUS IN PORTUGAL

When Christopher Columbus returned from his voyages in the North Atlantic in late 1477, he settled in Lisbon. At the time, Lisbon was rapidly becoming a wealthy and important center of trade. Merchants and seamen of all countries, including those from Italy, were drawn to Lisbon to share the wealth. King John II of Portugal was financing voyages to discover new islands and a passage to India by sailing around Africa.

Columbus's brother Bartholomew had recently moved to Lisbon. He worked for a business that produced charts for sea captains. He got Christopher a job there. Before long, the two Columbus brothers started their own chart-making business. The business was a success, as the brothers became very skilled at mapmaking. In those days, mapmakers had to rely on information brought to them by seamen. Countless conversations about sea routes must have taken place between the Columbus brothers and their clients.

When did Christopher Columbus first get the idea that one could reach India by sailing west across the Atlantic Ocean? Historians are not sure. In any event, Christopher Columbus was not the only person who believed that the earth was round and that such a route was certainly possible. At the time, every educated person knew that the earth was round.

When Columbus was in Iceland, already far west of continental Europe, he learned about lands even farther to the west—Greenland, and possibly Vinland, the Viking discovery in North America. Maybe that was when Columbus began thinking of an alternate route to the Indies. If one could sail west in the North Atlantic and eventually reach land, perhaps one could do the same by following a more southerly route across the ocean. Once Columbus began thinking about sailing west to the Indies, the idea stayed in the back of his mind. Indeed, it would eventually become an obsession.

In 1479, Columbus married Felipa Moniz Perestrello, a member of the Portuguese nobility. Her father, Bartolomeo Perestrello, had been governor of the Portuguese island of Porto Santo. After his death, Felipa's brother-in-law, Pedro Correa de Cunha, was named governor of the island. Porto Santo is located in the Atlantic, 27 miles northeast of Madeira. Columbus and Felipa moved to Porto

Santo in 1480 or 1481. Their son, Diego, may have been born there. Columbus's mother-in-law gave him her husband's collection of maps and navigation manuals that had been prepared for sea captains by Henry the Navigator's cartographers. As Columbus poured over this material, he learned all about Portuguese sea routes along the coast of West Africa.

Sometime between 1482 and 1484, Columbus sailed to Ghana and Guinea on the western coast of Africa. At Elmina in present-day Ghana, Columbus found a flourishing gold trade. He learned that there were two sources for gold. Near the coast, people found gold dust and nuggets by sifting river sand. Inland, they found gold by following veins in the rocks and digging vertical shafts. The Portuguese were importing significant amounts of gold each year. And individuals in the gold trade were becoming quite wealthy. Columbus decided that someday he would also become rich from the gold he hoped to find in the new lands he intended to discover.

# Chapter 3

# The Enterprise of the Indies

**When** Columbus sailed south along the coast of West Africa, he paid careful attention to the ocean currents and winds. He also perfected his navigational skills by studying the night skies and learning all the stars along his routes. As he sailed between the various island groups—the Cape Verde Islands, the Canary Islands, the Azores, and the Madeira Islands—he noted how conditions varied from place to place.

Columbus observed the phenomenon known as the Canaries Current, the ocean current running west from the Canary Islands. He also learned that the trade winds near the Canaries blew from the northeast all year long with the greatest regularity. Columbus realized that one could depend on these constant trade winds to push a sailing ship to the west. But if he were to somehow sail a ship thousands of miles across the ocean propelled by the trade winds, how would he ever be able to make the return voyage? After learning more about climate conditions in the Azores, Columbus had the answer to his question. In the latitude of the Azores, which is north of the Canaries, weather conditions are typically more unsettled. Winds are more variable and frequently blow from the west.

The more Columbus thought about the possibility of sailing west across the Atlantic to the Indies, the more convinced he became that he could make such a voyage.

## A BOLD PROPOSAL

To Europeans in the fifteenth century, the "Indies" included all lands east of the Indus River in Asia. These included present-day India, Myanmar (Burma), China, Japan, the Moluccas, and Indonesia. Not much was known about these distant lands and their rulers and cities except that they were the sources of exotic spices and jewels. The main source of information in Europe about the East was Marco Polo's book, which described many wonders of the fabulously wealthy kingdoms of China and Cipangu (present-day Japan).

In the middle of the fifteenth century, an event occurred that would create a huge obstacle to Europeans planning to trade with the East. In 1453, the Muslim Ottoman Empire captured the city of Constantinople (present-day Istanbul, Turkey). Constantinople had been the capital of the Orthodox Christian Byzantine Empire for centuries. It had been an important center of trade between Europe and Asia. Once the city fell under Muslim control, the ongoing centuries-long conflict between the Christian and Muslim worlds closed an important trade route from Europe to the East. If Europeans could discover a sea route to Asia, they could bypass the Muslims and gain direct access to the markets of the East.

Columbus was not a wealthy man. He knew that his voyage would cost a lot of money. He would need to find somebody willing to provide financing. His patron would probably turn out to be a European monarch motivated by the desire for a more convenient trade route to the Indies.

For Columbus, the time had come to put together his proposal. Probably the most important part of planning his voyage was to calculate the actual distances involved. Just how far was it from Portugal to the Indies? How long would such a voyage take? In those days, Europeans were not aware of the existence of the North and South American continents. And people also had no accurate idea about the actual width of Asia. Marco Polo had probably inadvertently exaggerated the overland distance from Europe to the eastern coast of Asia. He also claimed that Japan was about 1,500 miles east of China. So it is not surprising that experienced geographers and cartographers made mistakes. As did Columbus, since he relied on their estimates.

Columbus had learned about a physician and mathematician in Florence, Italy, named Paolo Toscanelli, who was especially interested in geography. According to historian Samuel Eliot Morison:

> Toscanelli, believing Marco Polo's estimate of the length of Asia to be correct, had written to a Portuguese friend in 1474, urging him to persuade the King to organize a voyage west to Japan, "most fertile in gold," and to the Chinese province of Mangi. He envisioned a voyage of 3,000 miles from Lisbon to Cipangu (Japan) and 5,000 miles from Lisbon to Quinsay (Hangchow), and sent a chart to demonstrate his theory.[1]

The letter including the chart, dated June 25, 1474, came into Columbus's hands about 1480. Columbus believed Toscanelli's distance estimates were true. He then estimated the distance from the Canaries to Japan to be 2,400 miles (actual distance is 10,600 miles) and the Canaries to Hangchow to be 3,550 miles (actual distance is 11,766 miles).

Columbus had known of others whose views supported his own beliefs. Aristotle was said to have written that one could cross the ocean from Spain to the Indies in a few days. Columbus had read *Geography*, the second-century geographic work by Ptolemy. Columbus possessed a copy of Pierre d'Ailly's *Imago Mundi (Image of the World)*, in which the author insisted that the ocean was "of no great width" between Morocco (on the northwest coast of Africa) and the eastern coast of Asia, and that it could be navigated in a few days with a fair wind.[2]

In 1484, his confidence bolstered by such support, Columbus arranged to present his plans to King John II of Portugal. John II, a nephew of Henry the Navigator, was interested in exploration

Columbus presents plans for a proposal for his first voyage.

43

and the discovery of new lands. However, he stopped short of promising to pay for Columbus's Enterprise of the Indies. Portugal had typically required sea captains to pay for their own voyages and rewarded them with titles or grants to land if they made discoveries. So John II did not respond well to Columbus's request for financing. Also, King John's geographers did not accept Columbus's distances and measurements. Finally, King John was committed to finding an eastward route to Asia by traveling around Africa.

According to the Portuguese historian João de Barros, in *Decades of Asia* published in 1552:

> The king, as he observed this *Christovão Colom* to be a big talker and boastful in setting forth his accomplishments, and full of fancy and imagination with his Isle Cypango than certain whereof he spoke, gave him small credit. However, by strength of his importunity it was ordered that he confer with D. Diogo Ortiz bishop of Ceuta and Master Rodrigo and Master José, to whom the king had committed these matters of cosmography and discovery, and they all considered the words of *Christovão Colom* as vain, simply founded on imagination, or things like that Isle Cypango of Marco Polo. . . .[3]

Although King John II rejected Columbus's proposal, the two parted as friends. There remained the possibility that at some future date, the king might reconsider.

## FERDINAND AND ISABELLA

In 1485, Columbus went to Spain to present his proposal to King Ferdinand and Queen Isabella. This was a difficult time for Columbus. His wife died that year. He moved to Spain, taking his young son, Diego, along with him. He hoped Ferdinand and Isabella would welcome his Enterprise of the Indies.

Columbus and his son sailed to Palos on the southern coast of Spain. At the nearby monastery of La Rábida, the friars agreed to take care of Columbus's son. Friar Antonio Marchena had studied geography and was eager to discuss Columbus's ideas. Marchena was very supportive of the plan to sail west in order to reach the East. Through Marchena and Friar Juan Pérez, Columbus eventually gained entry to the court of the Spanish monarchy.

Ferdinand and Isabella received Columbus at the royal court near Madrid on January 20, 1486. In presenting his plan, Columbus spoke forcefully with great conviction. He showed the royal couple a map of the world that he had made with his brother Bartholomew. The map depicted the lands Columbus intended to discover. Although Ferdinand was not inspired, Isabella found Columbus's ideas interesting. But the two were hesitant to make any commitment to Columbus at this time.

The learned men of their council did not believe that Columbus's ideas were valid. Furthermore, the Spanish rulers were preoccupied with the war in Granada in southern Spain, where they were trying to expel the Moors, Muslim conquerors of Spain.

King Ferdinand of Aragón and Queen Isabella of Castile were married in 1469, combining the

two most important kingdoms in Spain. Since the eleventh century, the Christian kingdoms in Spain had been waging a long and brutal war on the Muslims. King Ferdinand and Queen Isabella were determined to continue the war with the Muslims until the last one had been driven out of the Spanish Kingdom.

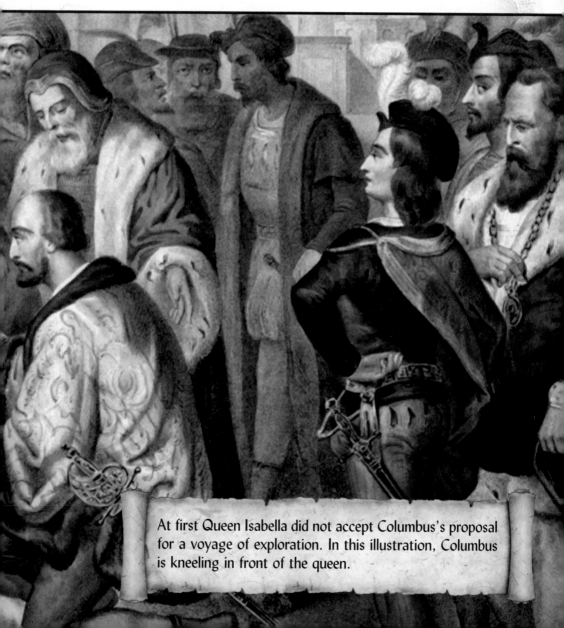

At first Queen Isabella did not accept Columbus's proposal for a voyage of exploration. In this illustration, Columbus is kneeling in front of the queen.

The Muslims had ruled Spain for hundreds of years. In the A.D. 700s, Arabs and other Muslim peoples from northern Africa conquered most of Spain and Portugal. The Muslim conquest began in 711, when Muslim armies crossed the Strait of Gibraltar and defeated the Visigoth king Roderic. The Muslims kept advancing until they were stopped by the Visigoth king Pelayo at Covadonga in northern Spain. The Muslim conquest was completed in less than two years, by the year 713.

The Spanish Muslims, called Moors, established a flourishing culture in Spain, especially in a southern region known as al-Andalus (Andalusia). The city of Cordoba became the cultural center of this area. The Moors had a more advanced culture than most of medieval Europe. They made important discoveries in mathematics, medicine, and other fields. They also preserved the writings of the ancient Greeks and Romans.

During the eleventh century, al-Andalus broke up into many smaller caliphates. The Muslims were weakened by rivalry among the caliphates. The Christian kingdoms in the north saw this as an opportunity to begin the *Reconquista* (Reconquest) of Spain. The struggle to drive the Moors out of Spain would last for several hundred years. Christians would retake a region only to be driven out once again by the Moors. Eventually the tide turned, and Christians gained the upper hand for control of Spain.

In 1487, Ferdinand and Isabella established the Inquisition in Spain. Pope Sixtus IV allowed them to appoint priests to hunt down heretics. A heretic was a person whose religious beliefs or practices differed from the teachings of the Catholic Church. People suspected of heresy were questioned and often tortured. When they confessed to being a heretic, they were often burned at the stake. Among the favorite targets of the inquisitors were Jews and Muslims who had converted to Christianity. Such people, known as conversos, were often accused of being false Christians. Anti-Semitism skyrocketed, and thousands of Jews were killed.

During this time of turmoil and tragedy in Spain, Columbus continued to hold out hope that Ferdinand and Isabella would approve his proposal. He prayed that they would take advantage of the opportunity he offered them. The council had examined Columbus's plan from November 1486 until April 1487. Columbus followed the royal court as it moved from Madrid to Avila to Guadalupe and then to Córdoba. In Córdoba, Columbus met and fell in love with Beatriz de Arana. In August 1487, Ferdinand and Isabella informed Columbus that they were rejecting his

plan. Still, he hoped that he might be able to win them over.

By early 1488, Columbus was growing impatient. He contacted King John II, who invited him to return to Lisbon and present his Enterprise proposal once more. Apparently, King John had dispatched the explorer Bartholomew Dias to attempt to reach India by sailing around the southern tip of Africa. But he had not yet received any progress report from Dias. In December 1488, however, Columbus was in Lisbon when Dias came sailing into the harbor. The Dias expedition had been a success. Now that Africa had been circumnavigated, the eastern sea route to India was open. King John II of Portugal would have no more use for Columbus. So Columbus returned to Spain.

While Columbus was still in Portugal, Beatriz had given birth to Ferdinand in August 1488. Columbus's second son was born out of wedlock. Although Columbus loved Beatriz, the two were never married.

In the spring of 1489, Columbus met with Duke Don Luis de la Cerda Medinaceli. When Columbus presented his plan, the duke was convinced of the importance and economic value of the Enterprise of the Indies. He immediately agreed to finance the expedition. He would provide the ships, crews, and whatever supplies were needed. But first he needed the approval of Spain's rulers. When the Duke informed Queen Isabella of his intentions, she refused to authorize the expedition. She said that such a major Spanish undertaking could only be sponsored by the monarchs.

In the summer of 1489, Queen Isabella met with Columbus again. She promised him that she and her husband would finance his expedition once they had expelled the last of the Muslims from Granada. So once again, Columbus was forced to wait.

On January 2, 1492, Ferdinand and Isabella's Christian army finally captured Granada, the last Muslim stronghold in Spain. Columbus took part in the monarchs' entrance into Granada. In the preamble to his journal, Columbus wrote: "I saw the royal banners of Your Highness rise over the towers of the Alhambra, and I saw the Moorish king come out of the city gate and kiss the hands of Your Highness and the prince."[4] The royal couple promptly issued the Edict of Expulsion, ordering all remaining Jews and Muslims in Spain to convert to Catholicism or leave. Any Jews or Muslims still alive who refused to convert were driven out of Spain.

Columbus looked forward to a quick approval of his plans by Ferdinand and Isabella. The royal couple were now the rulers of a newly united

Catholic Spanish kingdom. They were interested in expanding their power and spreading Christianity. They needed to find new sources of wealth to pay for an expedition to conquer Muslim-held Jerusalem. And they were jealous of Portugal's successes in establishing trading posts on the coast of West Africa and colonies in Madeira and the Azores.

Yet once again Columbus would suffer disappointment. The royal council met again to debate Columbus's proposal. Although some members were in favor of it, a majority were still opposed. While Columbus had waited patiently in Spain for the monarchs' approval, his brother Bartholomew had gone to England and then France. He had made presentations to the rulers of those countries, but did not have any success. Now Columbus, in desperation, thought about going to France himself to try to gain backing for his expedition.

However, the debate over Columbus's proposal was still continuing in the council chambers of the Spanish monarchs. Columbus's friends at the court had not given up. Father Fernando de Talavera, the confessor of Queen Isabella, had all along been against the proposal. His opinion carried a lot of weight in the council. As the debate continued, de Talavera began to waver. He realized that if Columbus received the support of another nation and his expedition was successful, then Spain would have been deprived of tremendous glory and riches. So de Talavera decided to recommend approval of Columbus's proposal, but insisted that the monarchs must be careful in order to minimize risk.

Ferdinand and Isabella were ready to finance Christopher Columbus's Enterprise of the Indies. A long negotiating process between the monarchs and Columbus finally resulted in an agreement known as the Capitulations of Santa Fe. The agreement was signed on April 17, 1492. Ferdinand and Isabella gave Columbus a letter of introduction to the Grand Khan of the Mongols, whom they hoped Columbus would meet soon after he arrived in China.

After signing the agreement, Columbus went to Palos. The southern Spanish port of Palos had been chosen as the expedition's point of departure. In Palos, Columbus would acquire three ships and assemble his crew and supplies. Before long, he would be sailing across the uncharted Ocean Sea.

# Chapter 4
# A Voyage to the New World

**During** the summer of 1492, Columbus was hard at work in Palos, Spain, preparing for his voyage. The people of Palos provided two caravels, the *Niña* and the *Pinta*. Each was about seventy feet long. The third ship was the *Santa Maria*, the flagship of the expedition upon which Columbus would sail. The *Santa Maria* was a type of ship known as a *nao*. This ship was somewhat larger and slower than the two caravels. It was about seventy-seven feet long and wider than the caravels.

There were many experienced seamen in Palos, but none seemed to be interested in signing up for the voyage. There were too many unknowns, and they did not like that the captain was a foreigner. But things changed once Martín Alonso Pinzón and his brother, two sea captains of Palos, agreed to sail with Columbus. The Pinzón brothers were well-regarded by the seamen of Palos. Once Columbus announced their participation, he had no trouble assembling the crews for the three ships. The crew of the *Santa Maria* included about forty seamen. The *Niña*

and the *Pinta* each had crews of about thirty men. Supplies, including enough provisions for a year at sea, were stored on the ships. The day of departure grew near.

## Sailing Across the Ocean Sea

Columbus and his three ships sailed out of the harbor at Palos on August 3, 1492. At the age of forty-one, Columbus's dreams were finally coming true. His long years of perseverance in winning sponsorship for his expedition had finally paid off. The fleet sailed south to the Canary Islands off the coast of West Africa. On September 6, the expedition departed the Canary Islands and sailed west. About five weeks later, on October 12, Columbus arrived in the Bahamas.

Columbus had become an expert navigator many years before his historic voyage across the Atlantic. In charting his course across the Ocean Sea, he relied on the compass and the astrolabe. The astrolabe was a metal disk inscribed with a map of the major heavenly bodies. On a clear night, it was possible to determine one's location by positioning the stars on the astrolabe to match the stars in the sky. In the uncharted waters of the Atlantic, Columbus mainly used a navigational technique known as dead reckoning. By starting with his ship's last known location, Columbus

Christopher Columbus bidding farewell to Queen Isabella of Spain on August 3, 1492. The boat Columbus is in would take him to the larger sailing ship, the *Santa María*.

would calculate the ship's direction, speed, and how much time had passed to come up with a new position.

Upon reaching the Bahamas, Columbus believed he had arrived in the East Indies. Although Columbus was an experienced navigator, he had made one big mistake. Of course, he knew the world was round. The notion that

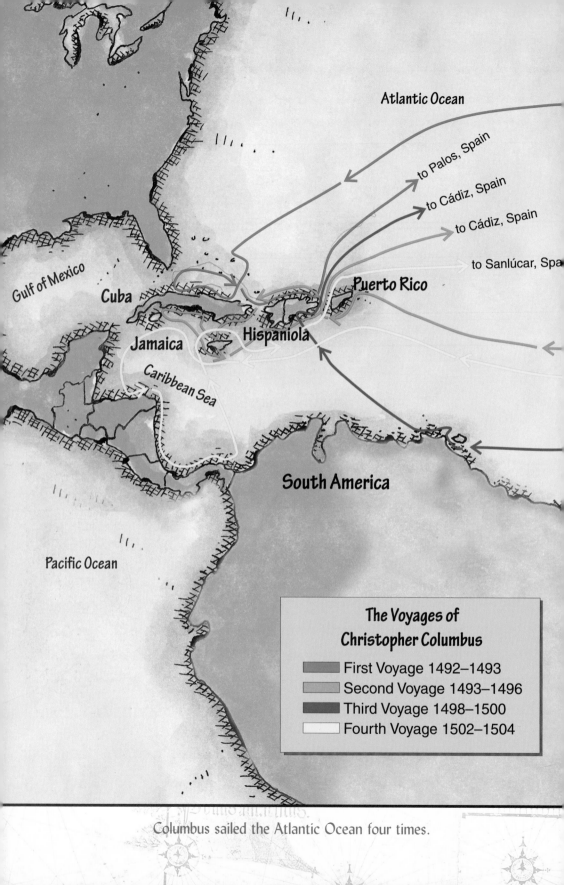

Atlantic Ocean

to Palos, Spain

to Cádiz, Spain

to Cádiz, Spain

to Sanlúcar, Spa

Gulf of Mexico

Cuba

Puerto Rico

Jamaica

Hispaniola

Caribbean Sea

South America

Pacific Ocean

### The Voyages of Christopher Columbus

First Voyage 1492–1493
Second Voyage 1493–1496
Third Voyage 1498–1500
Fourth Voyage 1502–1504

Columbus sailed the Atlantic Ocean four times.

Columbus was challenging a commonly held belief in a flat earth is a myth. And Columbus correctly assumed that he could reach Asia by sailing west. However, he had miscalculated the distance from Europe to Asia, believing the journey would be about three thousand miles. So after sailing westward across the Atlantic for three thousand miles, Columbus arrived in the Bahamas, not Asia.

Each year on October 12, many cities across the United States hold parades to commemorate Columbus's discovery of America in 1492. But did he really "discover" America? When Columbus first sailed west across the uncharted Atlantic Ocean, he landed on an island in the Bahamas. But he found people already living on the island. Columbus's "discovery" might better be called an "encounter." Indeed, the inhabitants called their island Guanahaní.

Above is an early form of an astrolabe. Columbus had this with him on his first journey, but it did not help him much because the waters of the Atlantic were mostly uncharted.

Columbus, believing he had arrived in the Indies, called the native Arawak "los Indios" (the Indians). Claiming the island for Spain, he renamed it San Salvador.

## THE ARAWAK OF THE CARIBBEAN

When the Ice Age ended, Paleo-Indians spread throughout the Americas. Some groups settled on the islands of the Caribbean Sea. These early seagoing peoples may have come from either Central or South America. Around 500 B.C., a people known as the Arawak arrived in the Caribbean. They came in very large canoes from the northern coast of South America. At the time, many of the islands were inhabited by the Ciboney, a hunter-gatherer culture. The Arawak were more advanced than the Ciboney. Wherever the Arawak settled, they tended to displace these earlier inhabitants. The Arawak of Hispaniola (the Caribbean island that includes present-day Haiti and the Dominican Republic), Puerto Rico, and eastern Cuba, were also called the Taino. Eventually the Arawak inhabited most of the islands of the West Indies. The Ciboney retreated to remote parts of the islands of Cuba and Hispaniola before disappearing altogether.

Meanwhile, the Arawak developed a successful agricultural and trading society on the islands.

Food was plentiful, and life was comfortable. The Arawak fished in the sea with woven nets. In addition to fish, the Arawak diet consisted of shellfish, iguanas, sea turtles, and hutia, a Caribbean rodent. The Arawak also grew many kinds of crops, including corn, yams, several types of grain, and cassava, a starchy root found in the tropics. Men smoked tobacco, rolled into cigars.

Trade was used as a means of promoting friendship and maintaining peace between islands. The Arawak traveled far and wide in order to trade with other peoples. They were skilled boat builders, navigators, and sailors. They made frequent trading voyages between islands, even traveling as far as the coastal villages of Mesoamerica, Florida, and perhaps South America. The Arawak used oceangoing canoes, some large enough to carry 150 men. They offered a wide variety of goods for trade, including cotton thread and fabric, pottery items, wood, gold, parrots, feathers, fruits, and other foods.

Each Arawak village was governed by a local leader known as a *cacique*. The Arawak villages competed with each other in ceremonial games played with a rubberlike ball on courts lined with standing slabs of stone. Among the most prized Arawak possessions was a low wooden bench carved in the form of a human figure lying down. Expert Arawak wood-carvers made this splendid

ceremonial seat, especially for caciques and other important people.

The Arawak villages were organized into chiefdoms, with up to eighty villages under the leadership of one paramount chief. The paramount chiefs maintained warehouses filled with goods for trade. Thus, they ensured their high status in the Arawak trade network. Trade was so important to the Arawak that children were taught at an early age that when you ask for something, you must be prepared to give something in return.

Arawak religion was based on a belief in personal guardian spirits, which each individual possessed. The power of a person's guardian spirit corresponded to the status of that individual within Arawak society. So the cacique and paramount chiefs would have the most powerful guardian spirits. The spirits of the chiefs were believed to be the gods of all the people ruled by the chiefs. Three-pointed carved stones, known as *zemis*, represented the spirits. The zemis were kept in temples and were believed to possess the powers of the spirits.

By A.D. 1400, the Carib, a new group of people from South America, had migrated to the Caribbean. The Carib chased the Arawak away from the southern islands. Almost a century later, many millions of Arawak still lived on the islands of the Caribbean. Some estimates suggest that as many as 7 or 8 million may have been living on the island of Hispaniola alone. But in the fateful year of 1492, none among the Arawak could have imagined the catastrophe that was about to envelop their world.

## COLUMBUS AND THE ARAWAK

The Arawak inhabitants of San Salvador greeted Columbus and his men with curiosity, friendship, and generosity. The Arawak, of course, did not call their island San Salvador. The name they used was Guanahaní. According to Columbus, the Arawak were "artless and generous with what they have, to such a degree as no one would believe but he who had seen it. Of anything they have, if it be asked for, they never say no, but do rather invite the person to accept it, and show as much loving-ness as though they would give their hearts."[1]

It seemed to Columbus that the Arawak regarded him and his crew as gods: "They believed very firmly that I, with these ships and crew, came from the sky; and in such opinion they received me at every place where I landed."[2]

However, two days after his arrival, still mar-veling at the generosity of the Arawak, Columbus wrote the following in his journal: "These people are very unskilled in arms . . . with fifty men they could all be subjected and made to do all that one

The Arawak took the small treasures that Columbus and his men gave them.

wished."³ Columbus immediately put his thoughts into action. He took some Arawak prisoners, demanding that they tell him whatever they knew about every valuable resource on the island. Then, learning that gold was not to be found on San Salvador, Columbus set sail to explore other nearby islands. At every place he landed, he claimed possession of Arawak lands and resources for Spain.

In December 1492, Columbus was sailing along the coast of Hispaniola when the *Santa Maria* ran aground on a coral reef. The ship was destroyed. But Columbus, his crew, and the cargo were saved by Guacanagarí, a friendly Arawak chief, and his people. Columbus and Guacanagarí exchanged gifts. Columbus gave the Arawak chief a red cape. Unfortunately, Guacanagarí made the mistake of giving Columbus several objects made of gold. He also mentioned that the source of the gold was nearby. Columbus was now more determined than ever to find the gold to enrich himself and the rulers of Spain.

Columbus established a settlement on Hispaniola called *La Navidad*. Leaving some of his crew there, Columbus sailed back to Spain. He took with him two dozen captive Arawak and a number of golden trinkets. He prepared a letter for the Spanish rulers, remarking that the Arawak "are fit to be ordered about and made to work, to sow and do [anything] else that may be needed."[4]

## ADMIRAL OF THE OCEAN SEA

On the return voyage to Spain, Columbus sailed aboard the *Niña*. He sailed north on the powerful ocean current known as the Gulf Stream and then caught the prevailing westerly winds. The *Niña* and the *Pinta* were separated in a storm before reaching the coast of Europe. Martín Alonso

The Arawak aid Christopher Columbus's crew in salvaging supplies from the *Santa María*, wrecked on a coral reef on Christmas Day, 1492. Columbus is speaking with a native, standing in the right foreground.

Pinzón and the *Pinta* landed at Bayona, Spain, while the *Niña* reached the port of Lisbon. There, the Portuguese authorities arrested Columbus. King John II accused Columbus of violating Portuguese sovereignty in the Atlantic. Eventually, Columbus was released, and he sailed away, arriving in Palos, Spain, on March 15, 1493. The *Pinta* pulled into Palos just a few hours after the *Niña*. Captain Pinzón was very ill and died shortly after.

When Columbus reached the royal court at Barcelona, he was invited to dine with Ferdinand and Isabella. He presented them with some gold objects and nuggets, and the Arawak he had brought with him. He told the royal couple that while he still expected to find a lot of gold for them, Arawak slaves could be a very profitable resource. Columbus also told Ferdinand and Isabella that the Arawak could be converted to Catholicism. Shortly after his initial encounter with the Arawak, Columbus had written: "I believe that they would become Christians very easily, for it seemed to me that they had no religion."[5]

When Columbus returned, he showed King Ferdinand and Queen Isabella what he brought back from his voyage.

The Spanish rulers were very impressed. They decided that the time had come to conquer the Caribbean and establish colonies. In the meantime, they awarded Columbus the title Admiral of the Ocean Sea as well as a substantial monetary reward. Columbus was also granted governorship of Spanish possessions in the Caribbean.

Meanwhile, the Portuguese suspected that Columbus might indeed have reached Asia. And he might have claimed for Spain lands that Portuguese sailors reached first. The rivalry between the two nations heated up. In May 1493, Pope Alexander VI suggested an imaginary line, the Line of Demarcation, drawn north to south through the Atlantic Ocean. All lands west of the line would belong to Spain. All lands east would belong to Portugal. When Portugal complained that the line gave too much to Spain, it was moved farther west, 1,100 miles west of the Canary Islands. The following year, an agreement known as

Columbus was rewarded with his own coat of arms. The castle and lion stand for royalty. The bottom left section shows the islands in the sea. The bottom right section stands for the Columbus family.

the Treaty of Tordesillas was signed by Spain and Portugal. The treaty confirmed Portugal's dominance in Africa—and later Brazil—in exchange for Spain's claim to the rest of the Americas.

# Chapter 5

# More Atlantic Voyages

**King** Ferdinand and Queen Isabella were serious about the conquest of the Caribbean. They outfitted Columbus's second voyage with seventeen ships, twelve hundred men, and thirty-four horses, as well as cannons, crossbows, guns, and attack dogs. This marked the beginning of the end for the unfortunate Arawak of the Caribbean.

## COLUMBUS'S SECOND VOYAGE (1493–1496)

On September 25, 1493, Columbus and his expedition left Cadiz, Spain, bound for the Canary Islands. Columbus's brothers Bartholomew and Giacomo accompanied him across the Atlantic. On the way to Hispaniola, Columbus discovered the islands of Guadeloupe and Puerto Rico. When Columbus returned to Hispaniola, he was shocked to find La Navidad had been burned to the ground and all of his men killed. The Arawak village of Guacanagarí had also been burned. The settlers who had just arrived with Columbus built a new settlement called Isabela, not far from La Navidad. Columbus placed

At the right of the map, Juan de la Cosa, navigator on the *Niña* on Columbus's second voyage, drew the coast of Europe. At the left, across the sea, he drew the coast of the New World as he imagined it to be. He painted it green, the color mapmakers use to show an unknown region.

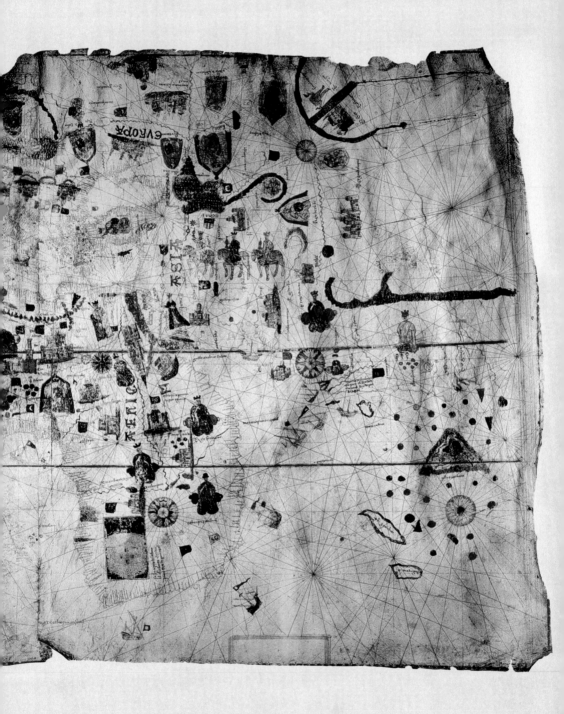

his brother Giacomo, who was using the Spanish name Diego, in charge of Isabela. Columbus then demanded that the Indians provide the Spaniards with food, gold, spun cotton, and other resources. The Spaniards forced the local Indians to work. Any Indian who disobeyed a Spanish command was likely to have his ears or nose cut off. Meanwhile, the settlers complained that Columbus's brother Diego was mismanaging the settlement.

By 1495, the Indians were fighting back. But Columbus waged all-out war on them. The Spaniards destroyed entire villages and burned alive, hanged, or enslaved their inhabitants. Columbus had not yet found significant gold deposits. Yet he needed to send something of value to the Spanish rulers. So he enslaved fifteen hundred Arawak and shipped five hundred of them back to Spain.

Ferdinand and Isabella did not exactly condone Columbus's policy of enslavement of the Arawak. The king and queen were only interested in converting the Indians to Christianity. And Christians could not be enslaved. But the Spaniards soon came up with a policy that permitted slavery. Any Indians captured in battle while rebelling against the Spaniards would be considered prisoners of war. And Indian prisoners, even those who had converted to Christianity, could be enslaved. From then on, Spanish leaders in the Caribbean found ways to provoke the Arawak into rebellion, thereby justifying their enslavement.

Columbus now demanded that the Indians bring him whatever gold existed on Hispaniola. In 1496, he set up a tribute system. Each Indian would have to deliver a specific amount of gold in a specified period of time. They would have to pan for gold in the streams and dig for gold in mines. Anyone who failed to deliver gold as required would have his hands cut off.

Columbus returned to Spain in 1496. Ferdinand and Isabella were aware of the settlers' complaints against Columbus and his brothers. But for now, they appeared grateful for Columbus's exploits and soon agreed to sponsor yet another voyage.

## COLUMBUS'S THIRD VOYAGE (1498–1500)

On May 30, 1498, Columbus sailed from Seville, Spain, with a fleet of six ships. Some of the ships were bound for Hispaniola. Columbus took the rest of the fleet to the Cape Verde Islands. From there, Columbus sailed across the Atlantic until reaching an island with three mountain peaks on July 31, 1498. The three large mountains reminded Columbus of the Holy Trinity, so he named the island Trinidad. Then he sailed south through the Gulf of Paria to the coast of South America. There he discovered the mouth of the Orinoco River.

On August 5, 1498, Columbus or some of his men set foot on the coast of Venezuela. This was probably the first landing of Europeans on the coast of South America. In his journal, Columbus wrote: "I believe this is a very great continent, until today unknown."[1] But he continued to

Christopher Columbus and his men discovered the three-peaked island of Trinidad in 1498.

believe that somehow, the "unknown" continent was a part of Asia. Columbus also believed that he had arrived at the threshold to the biblical Garden of Eden. Apparently, he was so struck by the beauty of the region that in his eyes it appeared to be a paradise on earth.

Columbus returned to Hispaniola as governor in late August 1498. He found that his brother Bartholomew had built a new settlement called Santo Domingo. It was located near some gold mines. Some of the settlers were rebelling against those loyal to the Columbus family. It would take two years to put down the rebellion.

Unable to bring peace to the settlement, Columbus appealed to Ferdinand and Isabella to send a judge to restore peace. The Spanish monarchs sent Francisco de Bobadilla, who was authorized to take over the governorship of Spain's Caribbean possessions from Columbus. Bobadilla seized Columbus's private property. He then arrested Columbus and his brothers and placed the three men in chains. In November 1500, Columbus arrived back in Spain, still in chains. Ferdinand and Isabella immediately ordered that Columbus and his brothers be freed. They ordered that any items taken from Columbus be returned to him, but they did not restore his titles. They did, however, replace Bobadilla with a new governor, Nicolás de Ovando.

Columbus in chains in a ship's hold on his way back to Spain after being arrested.

## COLUMBUS'S FOURTH VOYAGE (1502–1504)

When Columbus proposed his fourth voyage, Ferdinand and Isabella were easily convinced. In 1499, Vasco da Gama had returned to Lisbon after a successful trip around Africa and across the Indian Ocean to India. Now the Spanish monarchs were more interested than ever in finding a shorter sea route to the Indies by sailing west.

On May 9, 1502, Columbus set out from Cadiz, Spain, on his fourth and final voyage across the seas. He had under his command a fleet of four ships carrying one hundred fifty men. Accompanying Columbus was his brother Bartholomew and his son Ferdinand, who was now fourteen.

King Ferdinand and Queen Isabella, hoping to avoid trouble on Hispaniola, ordered that Columbus stay away from that island. They wanted him to focus on finding and bringing back anything that would add to their wealth—gold, silver, jewels, and spices. But Columbus, after a stop at Martinique, ignored the instructions from Spain's rulers. He arrived at Hispaniola on June 29, 1502, just as a hurricane was brewing. When he asked for permission to go ashore at Santo Domingo, the governor, Nicolás de Ovando denied the request. In his journal, an outraged Columbus wrote: "What man ever born, not excepting Job, would not have died of despair when in such weather, seeking safety for my son, brother, shipmates and myself, we were forbidden the land and the harbors that I, by God's will and sweating blood, had won for Spain?"[2]

Ignoring Columbus's warning about the weather, a fleet of ships set out from Santo Domingo for Spain. The next day, the storm struck

in all its fury, sinking almost all of the ships and drowning about five hundred seamen. Among these was Francisco de Bobadilla, the man who had previously sent Columbus back to Spain in chains.

When the weather cleared, Columbus sailed southwest to the coast of Central America. Columbus was sick much of the time. He suffered from rheumatism and ran a fever. His poor eyesight added to his discomfort. Along the coast of Panama, the weather was often stormy. One ship was lost in a particularly severe storm. The local Indians were hostile toward the Spaniards and eventually forced them to sail away. Columbus still hoped to find a passage to the Asian mainland. He grew discouraged when this goal never materialized.

In December 1502, Columbus headed back to Hispaniola. One of his ships had to be abandoned when it began sinking due to damage from small mollusks, known as sea worms. One hundred thirty men had to crowd onto the remaining ships. These ships, however, were also riddled with sea worms and were barely seaworthy. Columbus realized they would never make it to Hispaniola. Instead, they landed on Jamaica, about one hundred miles from Hispaniola. Columbus and his men were marooned there, dependent on the local Arawak for food.

The Indians eventually grew tired of supplying food to the Spaniards. Columbus had with him an almanac, which predicted an eclipse of the Moon. He told the Indians that he would punish them by taking away the light of the Moon. On the night of February 29, 1504, the Moon began to disappear during the lunar eclipse. The Indians agreed to continue providing their supplies of food.

Meanwhile, a seaman named Diego Méndez de Salcedo set out by canoe in an attempt to reach Hispaniola. He reached the island in five days. He eventually found Governor Ovando and told him that Columbus and his crew were stranded on Jamaica. Months later, Ovando sent a ship to check out Salcedo's story. Columbus and the shipwrecked sailors were rescued by the end of July and arrived in Santo Domingo on August 13, 1504. On September 12, Columbus, his son, and his brother arrived back in Spain. Columbus's fourth voyage had proved to be a disaster.

On November 26, 1504, while Columbus was recuperating at the monastery of Las Cuevas in Seville, Queen Isabella died. Columbus tried to regain his lost titles. In May 1505, King Ferdinand granted Columbus an audience. He did not return Columbus's titles, but agreed to give him 2 percent of the riches of the Indies. This was enough wealth to provide Columbus's family the lifestyle of the nobility.

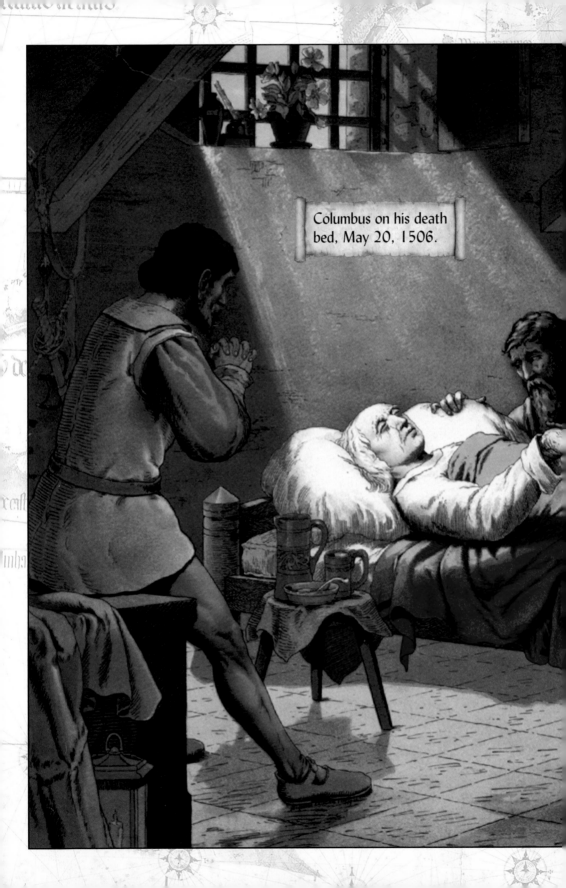

Columbus on his death bed, May 20, 1506.

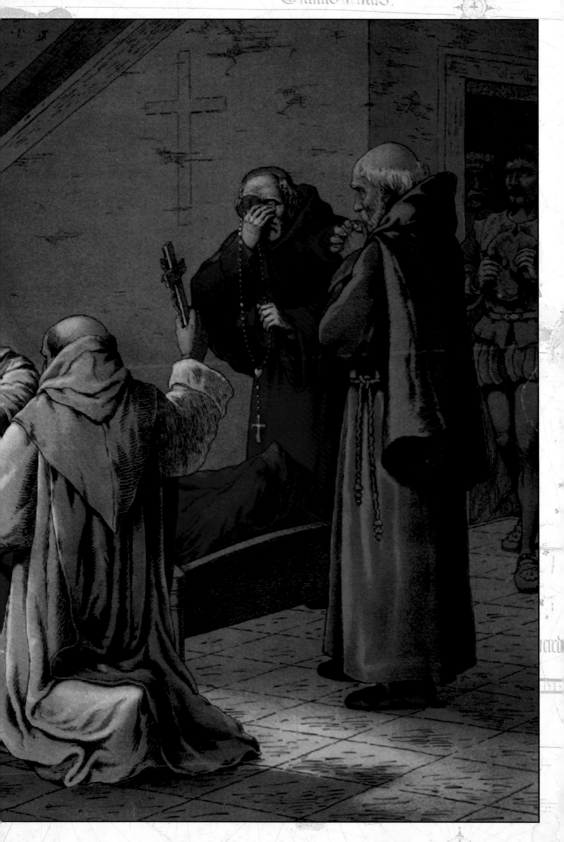

Columbus remained in the city of Valladolid until his death on May 20, 1506.

## COLUMBUS'S NAME

In the course of his four voyages, Columbus explored most of the Caribbean islands and sailed along the coasts of Central and South America. Until his death in 1506, he believed that he had reached Asia. But others knew better. Amerigo Vespucci, an Italian explorer from the city of Florence, sailed on a Spanish ship along the eastern coast of South America in 1499. He became the first person to publish the idea that a new continent had been discovered, in his widely circulated letter *Mundus Novus (New World)* in 1503.

Although Columbus had crossed the Atlantic Ocean before Vespucci, America was not named after him. Instead, in 1507, German mapmaker Martin Waldseemüller labeled the new land "America" on his map, in honor of Amerigo Vespucci.

While European cartographers failed to call the new-found lands Columbia, in honor of Columbus, his name has certainly not been forgotten. A 1988 survey determined that there were as many as sixty-five geopolitical entities in the United States using "Columbus," "Columbia," or some variation thereof in thirty-seven states (plus, of course, the District of Columbia), including fifty

84

cities, nine counties, five townships, and one air force base. This does not include the rivers, capes, mountains, falls, lakes, glacier, peak, and plateau, nor the many streets, avenues, highways, circles, bridges, parks, plazas, squares, and buildings. There is also a broadcast network, symphony orchestra, jazz band, string quartet, encyclopedia, movie company, colleges, railroads, banks, museums, journals, and a space shuttle, all named after a version of Columbus's name.

Outside the United States, "Columbus" or "Colon" or derivatives are used for one nation (Colombia), one national capital (Colombo, Sri Lanka, so named by the Portuguese in 1517), one major province (British Columbia), a series of small islands (in the Mediterranean, off Spain), an archipelago (in the Galápagos, where there are also places named after other figures associated with Colón, including Bartolomé and the Pinzóns), and towns and cities in every country of South America. In the English-speaking world, Christopher Columbus has given his name to more geographic places than any other actual figure in the history of the world, with the exception only of Queen Victoria; in the United States he surpasses all others except Washington.[3]

# Chapter 6

# CHANGING THE WORLD

The transatlantic voyages of Columbus would lead to an exchange of people, products (including plants, animals, and manufactured products), and ideas among three parts of the world—the Americas, Europe, and Africa. This so-called "Columbian Exchange" would have profound effects on the peoples of each continent. There would be political and economic effects as well as changes in lifestyle and changes to the environment. Some of the changes would be beneficial; others would prove to be devastating, even catastrophic.

## Exchange of Products

About half of all major crops now grown throughout the world originally came from the Americas. Such products included squash, sweet potatoes, white potatoes, avocados, peppers, chilies, maize (or corn), tomatoes, peanuts, cassava, manioc, pumpkins, pineapples, beans, peas, vanilla, and cocoa. Turkey and chocolate also came from the Americas. Another important product from the Americas was tobacco. Indians used tobacco mainly for ceremonial purposes. In Europe and in

Africa, the smoking of tobacco became highly fashionable.

Products introduced into the Americas from Europe included grains, such as wheat, oats, barley, and millet; vegetables, such as turnips, spinach, and cabbage; grazing grasses; and domesticated animals, including horses, pigs, cattle, oxen, sheep, goats, and chickens.

A number of important products that originated in Asia came to the Americas by way of Africa. Among these products were bananas, citrus fruits, rice, yams, sugarcane, and coffee. Such products became cash crops on plantations in the Americas. The exchange of food products among continents enriched human diets and made possible enormous population growth in many places.

There was also an exchange of manufactured products. Europe sent tools made of iron, sailing ships, wheeled vehicles, and firearms to the Americas. From the Americas came Indian hammocks, canoes, kayaks, snowshoes, and moccasins.

Unfortunately, another kind of exchange occurred between the three parts of the world—the exchange of disease-causing microorganisms. The effects of such exchanges were immediate and tragic. Many diseases that had long plagued Europeans did not exist in the Americas before Columbus's arrival in 1492. Europeans who came into contact with Indians often carried various disease-causing bacteria and viruses. Many Europeans had developed immunity to such contagious diseases as smallpox, measles, and typhus. But Indians had never before been exposed to such diseases. And they had never had the chance to build up an immunity to them.

Once Indians became infected with a particular disease, devastating epidemics soon swept through entire communities and regions. Even a relatively mild childhood disease, such as mumps, proved deadly to the Indians. Many historians believe that more than 90 percent of the Indian population of North America died of European diseases during the 1500s. If the estimated 1492 Indian population of 10 million is anywhere near accurate, the loss of Indian life was staggering.

Indians were not the only ones affected by the exchange of disease-causing microorganisms. Columbus's sailors became infected with syphilis in the Americas and carried the disease back to Europe. It spread throughout the continent, destroying hundreds of thousands of lives. Apparently, Indians were not as severely affected by syphilis as were the Europeans.

Another deadly disease that traveled to the Americas was malaria. This particular disease did not originate in Europe, but in Africa. While Africans seemed to have immunity to malaria,

Europeans and Indians did not. Malaria had a long history in Europe, going back to ancient times, especially in the Mediterranean area. Interestingly, a plant found in the Americas would provide the first-known effective treatment for malaria. In the late 1500s, Spanish doctors discovered that quinine, an extract from the bark of the South American cinchona tree, could cure malaria. Quinine was the first of many plants from the Americas that would prove useful in curing disease. Indeed, more than two hundred drugs today are derived from plants whose medicinal uses were discovered by American Indians.

## EXCHANGE OF IDEAS

The Columbian Exchange involved much more than just a swapping of products—plants, animals, and so forth—and diseases. Also traveling across the Atlantic in both directions were new ideas. The arrival of many European explorers, conquerors, and settlers in the Americas brought drastic changes to the lives of Indians wherever the two groups came into contact.

In many places, the Europeans enslaved the Indians. Age-old patterns of culture, sometimes thousands of years in the making, were destroyed almost overnight. Indians now had to do whatever was demanded of them by their European conquerors or suffer the consequences. Throughout the vast territories conquered by Spain, Spanish missionaries were determined to convert the Indians to Catholicism. Thus new ideas about religion and mankind's place in the universe were literally forced upon the Indians.

Meanwhile, news of Columbus's exploits in the Americas inspired tremendous changes in the thinking of many Europeans. In 1492, the Catholic Church had a powerful grip over all of Europe. Although for at least one hundred years, various voices had cried out for reform, change was slow in coming. But suddenly, many people were now beginning to question religious doctrine they had long accepted and taken for granted. Why, they wondered, was there no mention of Indians in the Bible? And for that matter, why didn't the Bible mention the Americas? The Catholic Church regarded as infidels those, such as the Muslims, who did not accept the teachings of Christianity. But the American Indians, for their part, had never rejected Christianity. They had just never before encountered it.

Once people began questioning aspects of church doctrine, it seemed logical to expand the scope of their inquiries. Religious thinkers, such as Martin Luther and John Calvin, attacked what they saw as corrupt practices of the Catholic Church. Luther and other reformers preached that salvation could be achieved without following

certain rules of the Catholic Church. The new doctrines became known as Protestantism.

The Protestant Reformation, the movement to reform the Catholic Church, began in 1517. That year, Martin Luther argued against the sale of indulgences by Catholic priests. An indulgence was a pardon issued by the pope absolving the purchaser of a particular sin. Luther preached that a sinner could be saved only by his or her repentance and faith in God's forgiveness, and not by the purchase of a pardon. According to Luther, the pope and church traditions were false authorities. People did not need priests to interpret the Bible for them. Many Europeans were drawn to the Reformation, and the authority of the Catholic Church was greatly weakened.

Information about the Americas would also have a profound effect on Europe's social and political philosophers. They were amazed that societies, such as the Arawak, could exist without a ruling monarchy in control. Some thinkers began to idealize such societies as being simpler and better than those of Europe. They imagined that such societies might have existed in Europe in the distant past. Of course, not all European thinkers agreed with this trend of thought. Many regarded Indian societies as primitive and undeveloped, and Indians as inferior to Europeans.

One European thinker, Sir Thomas More, was especially impressed with the Indians of the Americas. In 1516, he published his book *Utopia*, in which he described his ideas about an ideal society. He based his ideas on the social organization of the Inca Empire in Peru, an early version of a socialist welfare state. In *Utopia*, More complains that the idle nobles of Europe are rewarded while common laborers live miserable lives. But in Utopia, More's ideal society, all people do as much as they are able to do and get all that they need. Hundreds of years later, Karl Marx and Friedrich Engels theorized that "from each according to his ability, to each according to his needs," should be one of the guiding principles of an ideal Communist society.

## LONG-TERM EFFECTS OF COLUMBUS'S VOYAGES

Columbus's voyages led to the rapid exploration, exploitation, and colonization of the Americas. There were many immediate effects on both sides of the Atlantic. But the Columbian Exchange had such a great impact on the peoples of Europe, Africa, and the Americas that it resulted in profound long-term effects as well. Indeed, Columbus's discoveries would change the course of history in Europe, the Americas, and Africa.

The exchange of food products led to changes in diet and nutrition. But what was the result of changes in diet? When potatoes from the Americas were first introduced in Europe, many people were afraid they were poisonous and refused to eat them. Before long, however, attitudes changed. Potatoes provided a new source of food in many areas where food supplies had been scarce. The sudden availability of food in such areas led to an increase in population. During the 1500s and 1600s, there was a huge population explosion in Europe. Sadly, during this same period, the Indian population of the Americas was being decimated (by disease and other effects of the Columbian Exchange). At any rate, the population in Europe grew from about 81 million in 1500 to 100 million in 1600, and about 120 million in 1700. This in turn helped drive a European wave of immigration to the Americas.

The potato became a food staple in many parts of Europe. In places such as Ireland, the population would become largely dependent on the potato. Later, when the potato crop in Ireland failed, the resulting potato famine would cause a new wave of immigration to the Americas.

Meanwhile, the introduction of corn from the Americas to Africa had equally drastic consequences. Wherever corn was added to African diets, populations grew. The growing population of Africans helped fuel the African slave trade to the Americas. By the middle of the sixteenth century, gold mining and trading in the Gold Coast in Africa could not compete with the huge quantities of gold Europeans were extracting from the Americas. So by this time, slaves had become Africa's most profitable resource for European traders.

Throughout the 1500s, gold and silver from the Americas flowed into Spain and then other European countries. Political and religious leaders became fabulously wealthy. A powerful new class of merchants arose whose wealth and status derived from gold and silver rather than through ownership of land. The amassing of wealth would enable strong European nations to develop global trading networks. In their drive to exploit the resources of the Americas, however, European nations would compete with one another and often come into conflict. Eventually, Europe's wealth would lead to the rise of capitalism and the industrial revolution.

The building of colonial empires, a process set in motion by Columbus, would unfortunately encourage the development of racist attitudes. Previously, most Europeans had not had much contact with non-white peoples of other races. And Europeans, therefore, did not usually think of themselves in racial terms—of belonging to

the "white" race. But with increasing interaction with the peoples of the Americas and Africa, Europeans developed ideas about race. Europeans had been eager to exploit and enslave the peoples of the Americas and Africa. So it became convenient to regard non-whites as belonging to inferior races. The taking of land, wealth, and labor from the Indians of the Americas would lead to their near extermination. With the growth of racial prejudice, Europeans found it easy to justify black slavery. And the transatlantic slave trade created in the Americas a racial underclass of Africans and their descendants.

## EUROPEAN SLAVE TRADERS

During the 1400s, Portuguese traders in Africa were interested mainly in gold. But during the 1500s, the Spanish began shipping enormous quantities of gold to Europe from their conquered lands in the Americas. The relatively small amounts of gold available to traders in West Africa became less and less important. However, around this time, the Portuguese realized that Africa possessed another valuable resource—slaves. The Portuguese were aware that there was a growing market for slaves in the Spanish colonies and in the Americas.

When the Spaniards conquered and colonized various Caribbean islands, starting in Hispaniola, they had enslaved the local Indian peoples. Columbus himself remarked that "the Indians of this land . . . are its riches, for it is they who dig and produce the bread and other food for the Christians and get the gold from the mines . . . and perform all the services and labor of men and of draft animals."[1]

Unfortunately, although Columbus placed so much value on the island's "riches," he did little to protect the Indians. The Arawak were literally worked to death on Spanish plantations or digging for gold. The Spaniards then replaced them with shiploads of captive Indians from other islands. By the mid-1500s, of all the millions of Arawak who had inhabited the islands of the Caribbean, only a handful survived. Torture, murder, famine, and disease had taken their toll. By 1542, the Arawak population of Hispaniola was down to about two hundred. Eventually, brutal treatment and disease killed off most of the enslaved Indians. By 1552, there were no Arawak left on Hispaniola.

Bartolomé de Las Casas, a Spanish priest who came to the West Indies in 1502, was appalled by the Indian slave trade begun by Columbus. Las Casas believed that 3 million Arawak had perished after little more than a decade of contact with the Europeans. He wrote: "Who of those in future centuries will believe this? I myself who am writing this and saw it and know the most about

African slaves work on a sugar plantation.

it can hardly believe that such was possible."[2] And according to Las Casas, "What we committed in the Indies stands out among the most unpardonable offenses ever committed against God and mankind and this trade [in Indian slaves] as one of the most unjust, evil, and cruel among them."[3]

But according to sociology professor James W. Loewen, we "must not judge Columbus by standards from our own time. In 1493 the world had not decided, for instance, that slavery was wrong. Some Indian nations enslaved other Indians. Africans enslaved Africans. Europeans enslaved other Europeans. To attack Columbus for doing what everyone else did would be unreasonable."[4]

The Spaniards now had to turn elsewhere for slaves. And the obvious next source of slaves appeared to be Africa. The Spaniards began importing slaves from Africa to replace the Indians. The Portuguese traders in Africa seemed to be in the right place at the right time to profit from the trading of slaves.

Slavery, of course, was not something new in Africa. It had been well established in many parts of the continent for hundreds of years. In West Africa, many tribal societies depended on slave labor. Slaves were owned by rulers as well as by individual families. The commercial slave trade in Africa began when Arabs from North African lands traveled south and traded horses for slaves. Later,

Bartolomé de Las Casas was shocked and disgusted by the
Indian slave trade begun by Columbus.

Portuguese who already had established trade relationships with African rulers entered the slave trade. Many African rulers who had been selling slaves to Muslims and other African rulers saw little difference in selling slaves to Europeans. African merchants, with the help of these local rulers, captured Africans to be enslaved. They then delivered them to the Portuguese traders in exchange for gold, guns, and other goods.

Parade watchers attend the Columbus Day Parade between 44th Street and 72nd Street on 5th Avenue in New York City on October 10, 2005.

African rulers of small kingdoms in Guinea and Senegambia became very rich by providing slaves to the Portuguese. The Portuguese, in turn, became extremely wealthy by providing slaves to the Spanish colonies in the Americas. The business of buying and selling Africans expanded rapidly. Most of the slaves were victims of raids or wars between African kingdoms. However, many African rulers used the slave trade to get rid of people they considered undesirable, such as law-breakers or persons accused of witchcraft.

The first Africans began working as slaves in the Americas in 1511 in the mines on the island of Hispaniola. By the year 1600, as many as two hundred fifty thousand African slaves reached the Americas. Perhaps as many as fifty thousand died during the sea voyage from Africa. During the 1600s, the number of slaves shipped from Africa would increase dramatically. Eventually, the Spanish and then the Dutch, French, and English would also enter the slave trade. When the transatlantic slave trade finally ended in the 1800s, almost 12 million Africans had been shipped across the sea.

Today, descendants of the African slaves brought to the New World and of American Indians are understandably reluctant to celebrate Columbus Day. Yet this holiday is celebrated each year by millions of people in the United States. In

Landmarks of Columbus and his journey exist all over the world. This statue is in Barcelona, Spain.

April 1934, President Franklin D. Roosevelt proclaimed Columbus Day a national holiday. By 1938, Columbus Day was celebrated in twenty-two countries in Central and South America and in the Caribbean.

The course of history might have been different if Columbus had been a kinder, more generous man, and had he not been driven by the search for gold. However, Columbus did cross the uncharted Atlantic Ocean. He was not the only European to believe that the world was round. But he seems to have been the first to stake his life on it. And his voyages would change the world. He found lands previously unknown to Europeans and returned to tell about them, opening the way so that others could follow.

# Chapter Notes

## Chapter 1. The First Sight of Land

1. Robert H. Fuson, trans., *The Log of Christopher Columbus* (Camden, Maine: International Marine Publishing Company, 1992), p. 54.
2. Ibid., p. 62.
3. Ibid.
4. Ibid., p. 63.
5. Ibid., p. 66.
6. Ibid.
7. Ibid., pp. 66–67.
8. Ibid., p. 67.
9. Ibid., p. 69.
10. Ibid., p. 71.
11. Ibid., p. 72.
12. Ibid., pp. 73, 75.

## Chapter 2. Early Years at Sea

1. Kirkpatrick Sale, *The Conquest of Paradise: Christopher Columbus and the Columbian Legacy* (New York: Alfred A. Knopf, 1990), p. 51.
2. Paolo Emilio Taviani, *Columbus: The Great Adventure* (New York: Orion Books, 1991), p. 7.
3. Ibid.
4. Samuel Eliot Morison, *Admiral of the Ocean Sea: A Life of Christopher Columbus* (Boston: Little, Brown and Company, 1942), p. 18.
5. Ibid.
6. Ibid., p. 24.

## Chapter 3. The Enterprise of the Indies

1. Samuel Eliot Morison, *Christopher Columbus, Mariner* (Boston: Little, Brown and Company, 1955), p. 18.
2. Ibid., p. 19.
3. Samuel Eliot Morison, *Admiral of the Ocean Sea: A Life of Christopher Columbus* (Boston: Little, Brown and Company, 1942), p. 71.
4. Paolo Emilio Taviani, *Columbus: The Great Adventure* (New York: Orion Books, 1991), pp. 74–75.

## Chapter 4. A Voyage to the New World

1. Alvin M. Josephy, Jr., *500 Nations: An Illustrated History of North American Indians* (Grammercy Books, 2002), p. 114.
2. Ibid.
3. Ibid., p. 116.
4. Ibid., p. 123.
5. Ibid., p. 120.

## Chapter 5. More Atlantic Voyages

1. John Noble Wilford, *The Mysterious History of Columbus: An Exploration of the Man, the Myth, the Legacy* (New York: Alfred A. Knopf, 1991), p. 209.
2. Ibid., p. 237.
3. Kirkpatrick Sale, *The Conquest of Paradise: Christopher Columbus and the Columbian Legacy* (New York: Alfred A. Knopf, 1990), p. 360.

## Chapter 6. Changing the World

1. Herman J. Viola and Carolyn Margolis, *Seeds of Change* (Washington, D.C.: Smithsonian Institution Press, 1991), p. 13.
2. Ibid.
3. James W. Loewen, *Lies My Teacher Told Me: Everything Your American History Textbook Got Wrong* (New York: Simon & Schuster, 1995), p. 38.
4. Ibid., p. 74.

**Arawak**—Former native inhabitants of the islands of the Caribbean, called "Indians" by Columbus.

**astrolabe**—A metal disk inscribed with a map of the major heavenly bodies, used for navigating by the stars.

**caliphate**—The territory ruled by a Muslim leader, called a caliph.

**Canaries Current**—The ocean current running west from the Canary Islands.

**caravel**—A type of small, light, nimble sailing ship, such as the *Niña* and the *Pinta*, developed by the Portuguese.

**Carib**—A subgroup of the Arawak peoples of the Caribbean.

**circumnavigate**—To go completely around, especially by water.

**Columbian Exchange**—The exchange of people, products (including plants, animals, and man-made products), and ideas among three parts of the world—the Americas, Europe, and Africa—as a result of Columbus's voyages.

**Enterprise of the Indies**—Columbus's proposal for sailing west to reach the East.

**Guanahaní**—The Arawak name for the island in the Bahamas where Columbus first landed in the New World. He called it San Salvador.

**Hispaniola**—Present-day Haiti and the Dominican Republic.

**Indies**—All the lands east of the Indus River, including India, Burma, China, Japan, and Indonesia.

**Inquisition**—The systematic hunt for heretics in Spain, established by King Ferdinand and Queen Isabella in 1487.

latitude—A distance measured in degrees north or south of the equator.

Line of Demarcation—An imaginary north to south line down the middle of the Atlantic Ocean, 1,100 miles west of the Canary Islands.

meridian—Any line of longitude.

monopoly—Sole control of something.

Moors—Muslims from North Africa.

mutiny—An uprising or revolt, especially by members of a ship's crew or armed forces.

nao—A type of sailing ship somewhat larger than a caravel, such as the *Santa Maria*.

navigation—The method of setting the course of a ship.

Ocean Sea—The uncharted Atlantic Ocean.

Reconquista—The Christian reconquest of Spain from the Moors.

Sargasso Sea—A part of the Atlantic Ocean filled with weeds.

sovereigns—Kings or queens; supreme rulers.

Taino—A subgroup of the Arawak peoples of the Caribbean.

## FURTHER READING

Aronson, Marc and John W. Glenn. *The World Made New: Why the Age of Exploration Happened & How It Changed the World.* Washington, D.C.: National Geographic, 2007.

Collier, James Lincoln. *Christopher Columbus: To the New World.* New York: Marshall Cavendish Benchmark, 2007.

Doak, Robin S. *Christopher Columbus: Explorer of the New World.* Minneapolis, Minn.: Compass Point Books, 2005.

Dugard, Martin. *The Last Voyage of Columbus.* New York: Little, Brown and Company, 2005.

Freedman, Russell. *Who Was First?: Discovering the Americas.* New York: Clarion Books, 2007.

Wulffson, Don. *Before Columbus: Early Voyages to the Americas.* Minneapolis, Minn.: Twenty-First Century Books, 2008.

## INTERNET ADDRESSES

**Introduction to 1492: An Ongoing Voyage**
  <http://www.loc.gov/exhibits/1492/>

**The Mariners' Museum—"Age of Exploration: Christopher Columbus"**
  <http://www.mariner.org/educationalad/ageofex/columbus.php>

**Medieval Sourcebook—Christopher Columbus: Extracts from Journal**
  <http://www.fordham.edu/halsall/source/Columbus1.html>

# Index